W9-AUM-651

EARLY AMERICAN
FOLK & COUNTRY ANTIQUES

EARLY AMERICAN
FOLK & COUNTRY ANTIQUES

by DONALD R. RAYCRAFT

Foreword by MARY EARLE GOULD
Sketches by CAROL M. RAYCRAFT
Photographs by RICK IMIG & JERRY HYMAN

CHARLES E. TUTTLE COMPANY: PUBLISHERS
Rutland, Vermont

Representatives
Continental Europe: BOXERBOOKS, INC., Zurich
British Isles: PRENTICE-HALL INTERNATIONAL, INC., London
Australasia: PAUL FLESCH & CO., PTY. LTD., Melbourne
Canada: HURTIG PUBLISHERS, Edmonton

Published by the Charles E. Tuttle Company, Inc.
of Rutland, Vermont & Tokyo, Japan
with editorial offices at
2-6, Suido 1-chome, Bunkyo-ku, Tokyo, Japan (112)

First edition, 1971
Third printing, 1975

Library of Congress Catalog Card No. 70-142778
International Standard Book No. 0-8048-0961-5

PRINTED IN JAPAN

This book is dedicated to

D J R

Who inspired the uninspirable

to care

CONTENTS

PHOTOGRAPHS

Country Furniture

Country Kitchen Antiques

Early Artificial Lighting

Potpourri

Country Store Antiques

SKETCHES

FOREWORD
By Mary Earle Gould

My interest in early American folk antiques dates back to the fall of 1932 when, quite unenthusiastically, I accompanied a collector friend and found an old cheese box in an up-country shed that appealed to me as an ideal container for my rag-rug paraphernalia. Of added interest was the yellow lettering on the bottom, "S. Reed," the name of its former owner who, as it turned out, had lived at one time in the childhood home of my father.

It was not too long before I became completely fascinated with all kinds of primitives, particularly wooden and tin ware, not only as treasures to be hunted for and collected, but as artifacts constituting an integral part of the cultural environment of our ancestors, about which very little had been written. Henceforth I devoted all of my energy to the arduous task of exploring this interesting and challenging facet of American social history, and I have been overwhelmed by the enthusiastic response to my efforts. It is most gratifying to see the growing interest of everyday American citizens in learning about, living with, and writing about their "Early American Folk and Country Antiques," and I am happy that such people as Donald R. Raycraft will carry on where we left off.

Chapter One

INTRODUCTION

THE PRIMARY PURPOSE behind the writing of this book is to provide some insight for the reader into the field of country antiques as it exists today. The author's aim is to include information that has utility for both the neophyte and the advanced collector.

The author has read the majority of works published during the past several years that are concerned with country and early American antiques, all of which have been found to be interesting and stimulating. It is primarily because of this stimulation that work was started on the present volume, *Early American Folk and Country Antiques.*

After reading an especially interesting and well illustrated book about early American furniture and gazing longingly at the pictures that accompany the text, the reader is stimulated to search for a duplicate of that particular Windsor chair, dry sink, or piece of early artificial lighting that has caught his fancy. He will probably find himself with the same dilemma that faced the searchers for the storied Holy Grail when he attempts to find a similar example for sale.

My wife and I, as collectors, are most interested in pieces that we might find and add to our home at reasonable prices. We certainly appreciate the fine example of a 17th-century corner cupboard shown in a Wallace Nutting book, but we are aware of the sad fact that we probably will never own one or even be fortunate enough to see one for sale.

On the following pages we have attempted to put together pictures and descriptions of country furniture, country kitchen utensils, early examples of artificial lighting, and country store items that are still being found for sale at antique shows and shops.

Several of the pieces described and illustrated possibly may already be a valued part of your collection or in the antiques shop around the corner. It is also possible that some may be found only after a search of several years duration.

The items described and depicted in the following chapters are from the author's personal collection or borrowed from the homes of friends. We are especially grateful to Mr. and Mrs. John Curry of Mahomet, Illinois who opened their home and their extensive knowledge of early Americana to us.

Figure 1. Foot stove. Illustrated here is an early nineteenth century foot stove or foot warmer. The foot stove was used in open sleighs and during all-day sessions in church. A small tin pail inside the stove contained hot coals that kept the user's feet warm. The majority of the foot stoves were made of tin framed in pine. The pierced tins allowed the heat to escape. The earliest stoves were made completely of wood.

Chapter Two

ON COLLECTING COUNTRY ANTIQUES

FOR THE PURPOSES of this project, country antiques may be defined as the typical household furnishings of rural and frontier America in the 18th and 19th centuries.

This operational definition grants us much freedom in the examples we have chosen for inclusion. During the years following the Civil War much of the household furniture and accessories were mass-produced in factories. Many of the factory-made articles are collector's items today. Factories turned out many products in the years stretching from 1865 to 1900 that are finding their way into homes and antique shops today.

Country furniture and country accessories are almost impossible to date accurately because the same fundamental designs were used in construction for almost a century and a quarter. Rural America in the 18th and early 19th century was primarily concerned with carving out a living in a youthful and difficult land. Much of the furniture in the home was made from lumber that was cut within a few miles of the home. It appears that the basic simplicity and functional design of the furniture illustrate the point that a nation and a people who are laying the foundations of a civilization have little time or inclination for involved and needless decoration in their household furnishings. This concern with ornamentation was to come in the late 19th century with the Victorian Age. The rural people of the eighteenth century built their furniture to endure and serve a specific function within their homes.

The authors choose to use the terms "country" and "folk" in describing the furniture and accessories rather than "primitive."

Folk furniture, like folk music or folk art, was produced by the common man of rural or small-town America. The simplicity of a folk song and the basic simplicity of a pine dry sink or butter churn go hand in hand. Each was developed to meet a need. The composer of the song, like the maker of the dry sink, has long since been forgotten, but his creation lives on, still bringing satisfaction and pleasure to its user.

The primary source for collectors of country antiques today is the antique shop. The idea of purchasing rare bargains at country sales has almost been erased. It is possible from time to time to happen upon an unusual piece of furniture, but the amount of time spent in taking in the sales is hardly worth the effort expended. It is also very probable that the piece purchased at a country sale will be "in the rough," that is, it will be covered with several generations of paint and may be in need of serious structural repair. Most country sales today seem to feature early Montgomery Ward.

The reader is advised to become familiar with the shops in his area and to talk to the dealers about their merchandise. The best source in your area is the dealer who specializes in country antiques. He is probably a dealer-collector who will be happy to share his knowledge with you. The general line shops (shops that stock a variety of antiques from glassware to barbed wire) may periodically have an individual piece or two, but the specialist is the most knowledgeable and has the largest supply of quality and authentic country antiques.

Many antique shops advertise "primitives" along with glassware and furniture. These "primitives" are usually in the basement, and generally consist of post World War I meat grinders and similar merchandise at inflated prices.

Geographically the eastern section of the United States is still the nation's chief repository of the really good country antiques. Most of the country furniture found around the rest of the country had its origin in Pennsylvania, New York State, or New England. The Atlantic coast states and Ohio are additional fertile areas for collectors. The dealers in the rest of the country who sell country antiques obtain much of their stock in the East. Thus the cost of the buying trip and a profit margin have to be added to the piece you may find in a local dealer's shop. The collector is advised to eliminate the middleman if possible, and go directly to the source to find the best in buys. A valid rule of thumb exists in regards to quality, quantity, and cost of country antiques: The farther west from Pennsylvania and New York State one travels, he will note a steadily increasing price and an equally steady decrease in quantity and quality. This is obvious when the traveler considers the east-west migration pattern in which our country was initially settled. From the establishment of the Plymouth Colony in 1620 to the granting of Illinois' statehood in 1818, a period of almost two hundred years transpired and only half of the continent had been traversed.

Trends in Prices

It would appear that the upward trend in prices and a corresponding decreasing supply of quality antiques in the market place will continue. The increasing awareness of people concerning our nation's heritage has brought about thousands of new collectors. This awareness is coupled with a desire by many people for informality in their household furnishings.

As quality country antiques go off the market, dealers are finding it increasingly difficult to restock their shops. In his classic *Colonial Lighting* Arthur Hayward wrote in 1923 ". . . almost any dealer will tell you today that the difficulty is not in selling his stock, but in replenishing it. The demand has overtaken the supply." Over forty years ago Hayward made the point that the supply of genuine antiques cannot increase. He also suggests that the supply is actually decreasing yearly through fire, decay, and accidents.

The diminishing supply of country antiques is accelerated by a constantly increasing number of potential buyers. Mr. Hayward summed it up when he comments ". . . under these conditions what better of safe use is there for your spare change than an intelligent, conservative investment in some form of antiques."

The number of attics that were once veritable storehouses for countless treasures of an earlier age can now be counted on two or three hands.

Price Guides

There are a number of price guides for sale in book stores today. Many are published annually at a cost of five to nine dollars. Personally, I place little faith in these various guides and suggest that the best price guide is *The Antique Trader,* a newspaper of advertisements published weekly from Dubuque, Iowa. The basic problem with price guides is that they attempt to survey the entire field of antiques.

We find price guides for the most part to be unrealistic and outdated shortly after they are issued. The *Trader* contains literally hundreds of ads from dealers and collectors all over the country in each issue. This gives the reader an opportunity to note the various prices asked throughout the nation for the same item. Price guides have a tendency to be sectionally orientated rather than national in outlook. The reader may also buy with assurance through the mail from the advertisers.

The final pages of each issue are devoted to a listing of outstanding sales, shows, and auctions scheduled around the country.

Chapter Three

COUNTRY FURNITURE

COUNTRY FURNITURE is becoming increasingly popular among people who are desirous of informal and unique surroundings in their homes. The collector today may find that a beautifully refinished 19th-century dry sink is less expensive in an antiques shop than a reproduction in the local furniture store. The antique will increase significantly in value through the years, and the newly made piece will take the opposite road. The country furniture will also provide self satisfaction to the owner for he may be assured that he probably has a one-of-a-kind piece of hand-crafted furniture.

The buyer of country furniture must be wary of purchasing newly made pieces masked as antiques. There is no single method of detection that keeps even the most knowledgeable buyer from being clipped on occasion. However, there are a number of precautions that may be taken. Probably the best single safeguard a buyer can take before purchasing a country antique is to do some research prior to entering the marketplace. There are countless books in print that describe all antiques from the rarest to the most common. A buyer should also try to deal with shop owners he knows personally or who have a good reputation. The best education an antiques collector may obtain is to temper his readings with short trips to many antiques shops. From viewing the dealer's merchandise and talking with him much can be learned. The buyer, however, should not automatically assume that a dealer is an authority merely because he is in the business.

Antiques have been reproduced since the first collector happened down the street. Today many of these reproductions, made forty to fifty years ago, are being sold and accepted as the real thing. Arthur Hayward describes an incident of finding a large number of pierced-tin candle lanterns in several shops. He reports the lanterns "... should be collected with considerable caution as they are comparatively easy to counterfeit." He suggests that the appearance of age can be added to the lanterns by burying them in moist earth and treating them with acid. Simulated antique furniture can be reproduced just as easily with aged wood and ancient hardware. Mr. Hayward's comment was made in 1923 when his book was first published. In the almost fifty years since the lanterns he mentioned were made, they have probably taken on additional marks of age that would brand them unquestionably as being eighteenth-century in origin. Exactly the same is true of individual pieces of furniture reproduced over the years.

There is a variety of examples of country furniture the collector may find available today. This chapter will include illustrations and descriptions of the following forms of country furniture: tables, kitchen cupboards, hutches, dry sinks, chairs, rocking chairs, benches, bins, and pie safes.

When one goes in search of a particular piece of country furniture he should keep in mind that antiques shops have no standard retail prices for their wares. The potential buyer should not hesitate to ask the shop owner if the figure on the price tag is the selling price or the asking price. Often a dealer will discount his asking price from ten to twenty per cent to make a sale.

Dry Sinks

Included on the list of items covered in this chapter are two the reader may not readily be familiar with: dry sinks and pie safes. A dry sink is a rectangular box-like affair constructed originally to hold the household wash bucket and wash utensils in days prior to indoor plumbing. The sinks were also used to wash the family dishes. Dry sinks are among the most sought-after pieces of country furniture today. When found in the rough, most of the

Plate 1. Mid-19th century pine wood dry sink from Ohio.

sinks still have the zinc liner in the recessed trough on the top of the sink. Dry sinks with a high back or splash board and drawers are becoming increasingly difficult to find. Sinks are found in walnut, oak, poplar, and pine. The sinks were used throughout the 19th century and, surprisingly, well into the 20th century.

Decorators today replace the zinc lining with sheet copper and use the dry sink as a planter, bar, serving piece, or to house a stereo complex.

Plate one is typical of many hand-crafted sinks that are still being found. The zinc liner from this sink has been removed. The small shelf on the splash board probably is not original and was added at a later date. Sinks of this type were made from about 1840

Figure 2. Dry sink, circa 1870. This has an unusually high splash board and a single drawer. The purpose of the high back is obvious when one considers the use sinks were put to. The storage area underneath the sink was used to store washday tools. Dry sinks with drawers are not common.

through 1870. After 1870 many commercially-made sinks began to appear. Dry sinks often were built into homes along with the kitchen cabinets in the later 19th century. The unusual hutch dry sink shown in Plate 2 is from Pennsylvania. A number of authorities on country furniture define a hutch as a chest or cupboard, often with open shelves, that is used primarily for storage. They

Plate 2. Pine hutchdry sink, early 19th century.

also agree that a hutch must have two drawers at the bottom and a like width at the top and base of the piece.

This hutch-dry sink was used in a country kitchen to display the family dishes and pewter.

The back of this piece is made of five boards of varing width. This aids to some degree in approximating a date for it. Later 19th-century cupboards and factory-produced furniture have a back made from a single piece of wood cut to size. The country craftsman who made the hutch-dry sink above used the wood he had at hand.

Pie Safes

Pie safes are kitchen pieces that were used to store pies and baked goods fresh out of the ovens of countless country kitchens in the mid-19th century. The doors of the safe and often the sides contain pierced tin sheets framed in wood. The safe is normally off the ground from six to eight inches on legs. The elevation was important in keeping out household pests. The doors often contain examples of early American folk art with hand-punched or pierced-tin sheets. This allowed the pies to cool and air to circulate within the safe. Countless designs, both hand-worked and machine-stamped, may be found on the tin sheets. Pie safes are considered to be a mid-western product dating from about 1850 to the first decade of the 20th century. The value of a safe is determined by how unusually the tins are decorated. Tins with pierced designs of animals, birds, household utensils such as coffee pots, unusual floral or geometric designs, and hearts are especially choice pieces.

The unusual pine safe pictured in Plate 3 contains hand-pierced tins. This safe, in addition to providing a ventilated upper section for food storage, has a middle drawer for kitchen utensils, and a large bottom storage area.

The factory-stamped tins and the hand-punched tins are easily differentiated. A factory-stamped tin in a pie safe will be identical to the other tins in the safe. No hand-pierced tins will ever be identical to the others in a pie safe. The factory-stamped tins date

Plate 3. Pine pie safe, mid-19th century.

from about 1870. The earliest safes have the tins nailed to the outside of the safe doors rather than framed within the wooden doors.

Occasionally one will happen across a pie safe with window screening in the doors and on the sides rather than tin sheets. These safes are of a later period and were used into the 20th century. Their value is much less than the earlier pie safes with pierced-tin doors.

TEXT CONTINUED ON PAGE THIRTY

Plate 4. Walnut and poplar pie safe, circa 1860. This has unique pierced-tin doors in the shape of a "Saint George" cross. It came from a minister's home in southern Indiana.

Plate 5. Poplar and pine factory-made pie safe. A typical midwestern pie safe that dates from about 1880. The geometric design on the tins was stamped by a machine. The tins are framed within the doors. Like many factory-period examples, this piece is constructed of several woods. Pie safes "in the rough" can often be found quite reasonably.

The most difficult job in refinishing a safe with several coats of paint on it is cleaning the tins. The tins should be removed from the doors if possible and soaked in a mixture of lye and water. Often each hole has to be individually hand punched with a sharp object and a hammer.

There is a geographical factor connected with the availability of several types of country furniture. As mentioned previously, pie safes are more commonly found in the middle west than in any other section of the country. Jelly cupboards, hutch tables, and Windsor chairs are seldom seen in large numbers outside of Ohio, Pennsylvania, New York State, and New England.

Factory-produced kitchen cabinets with a multitude of drawers and bins were common in the homes of the late 19th-century and early 20th-century America.

Kitchen Cabinets

The tops of many of the cabinets are detachable and merely rest on their bases. The buyer will occasionally see the upper half of a kitchen cabinet displayed and sold by itself. Many people remove the large bottom bins and convert the cabinet into a desk. Kitchen cabinets were advertised in numerous mail-order catalogues and sold for from ten to sixteen dollars in the years between 1880 and World War I. The example in Plate 6 has turned legs and two pull-out bread boards.

The typical factory-produced kitchen cabinet was inexpensively constructed and mass produced. Those that are still being found often have warped drawers and other similar structural infirmaties brought on by age. They are found heavily painted and badly in need of refinishing.

There is a variety of styles of cabinets ranging from the plain one shown in Plate 6 to glass-doored cabinets of white oak. The majority were constructed of pine or maple. The cabinets made in the first quarter of the 20th century are taller and not as wide as the earlier ones. Many of them do not have the large flour bins. The working tops are made of porcelain or aluminum rather than

Plate 6. Pine kitchen cabinet, late 19th century.

wood. The knobs on the doors are made of white ironstone. The stoneware cookie jar on the left in Plate 6 was made and signed in Bennington, Vermont. The circular wooden plate at right is a late 19th-century factory-made bread board.

Plate 7. Pine cattle salt lick, probably 19th century.

Salt Licks & Milking Stools

The unique pine log pictured in Plate 7 was used by a New England farmer to store salt for his cattle. The salt lick was put in the field or by a watering trough for the cattle to sample as they chose. It is practically impossible to date, though its construction would suggest that it is 19th century in origin. Like many pieces of unusual country furniture, this piece has a number of decorating possibilities for the 20th-century home. It is crude, yet its weather-beaten exterior contains significant beauty for the collector of country antiques.

Rocking Chairs

The rocking chair is considered to be an American invention. Ben Franklin is often given credit for adding rockers to a straight chair to form the first rocking chair. 18th-century rocking chairs for the most part are reconditioned straight chairs. The placement of the chair legs on the rockers gives some indication as to the age of the chair. The earliest chair had an equal length of rocker in front of and behind each chair leg. Later rocking chairs have legs attached toward the front of the rockers.

Figure 3. This illustration shows rockers from the 18th and early 19th centuries. The one on the right dates after 1830.

Two basic kinds of rocking chairs are available today, the Boston rocker and the Salem rocker. Both were first made during the middle decade of the 19th century. The Boston rocker has a scrolled or rolled seat and arms. The Salem rocker has a flat seat and arms.

The Boston fiddleback in Plate 10 is painted black with a red seat. The original floral decoration adds much to the attractiveness

Plate 8. Milking stool, 19th century.

TEXT CONTINUED ON PAGE THIRTY-EIGHT

Plate 9. Boston fiddleback rocker, circa 1850.

Plate 10. Maple and pine spindle-back rocker.

Plate 11. Pennsylvania balloon-back rocker. This one dates from the first third of the 19th century. It was found in Galena, Ill., the hometown of U.S. Grant. The "cricket" is actually a salesman's sample meat block from the early 20th century. "Crickets" were popular in the seventeenth century to keep a tired citizen's feet off the cold and drafty floor while he rested in his favorite chair.

Plate 12. Boston child's rocker. 19th century. This one is constructed of maple and poplar, with a pine seat.

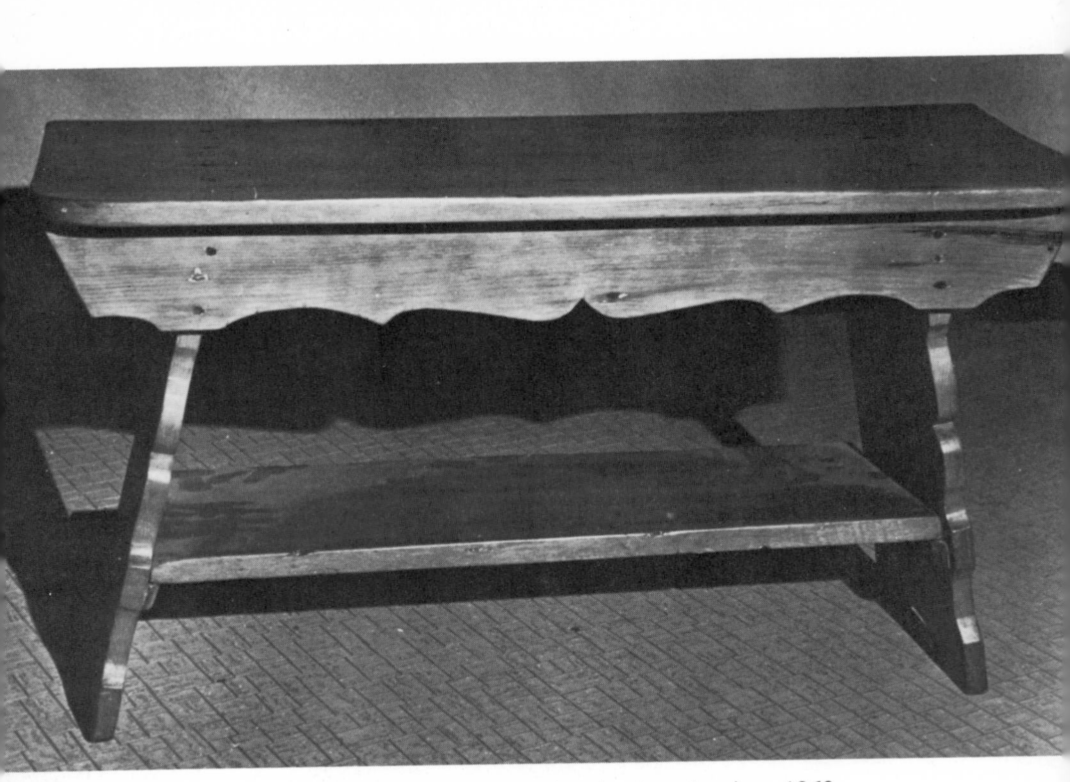

Plate 13. Pennsylvania pine bench, circa 1860.

of the chair. This rocker is called a fiddleback for obvious reasons. The chair is constructed chiefly of maple.

The fiddleback rocker is said to be a mid-western innovation. The particular Boston fiddleback illustrated here was sold by Cougle Brothers General Commission Merchants of South Water Street, Chicago, Illinois. The Cougles also dealt in butter, eggs, cheese, poultry, veal, dressed hogs, game, hides, wool, and tallow. They marketed this particular chair for $2.50.

The chair in Plate 9 dates from about 1840. The first colonists learned that each tree in the forest had a job it could best perform. Seldom is a chair found that is made from a single type of wood.

In addition to the rockers illustrated there are a number of other basic forms the collector may still find. A smaller Boston rocker with no arms was used by mothers nursing their children. The nursing rocker is also called a sewing rocker.

Possibly the most uncommon form of the rocking chair is the mammy's bench. A mammy's bench is similar to a deacon's bench with rockers attached. A small "gate" was attached to the bench that protected the sleeping infant from rolling onto the floor. The mother was able to rock her child while doing simple household tasks or sewing.

Benches

Benches in various stages of repair or erosion are frequently found. Most of them were made of pine and are of the wash-bench variety. Wash benches were used on the back porch of country homes to serve as a depository for buckets and scrub or wash

Plate 14. Pine wash bench with "boot-jack" legs, 19th century.

Plate 15. Deacon's bench, 19th century.

boards. The typical wash bench found today will be covered with several generations of paint. Many of the benches need serious structural repairs because of lengthy exposure to the weather. Wash benches are normally eighteen to twenty inches high. Benches made for sitting and use in the home were a little higher.

Benches used as pieces of furniture in country homes are more decorative and less common than the wash bench. The pine bench shown in Plate 13 has attractively scalloped legs and front apron. The ledge is removeable and adds to the beauty and utility of the bench.

The deacon's bench is also variously known as a settee or settle. The example illustrated in Plate 15 has a pine plank seat and maple legs. The spindles are hand-turned. The name "deacon's bench" that is applied to all 20th-century reproductions is a misnomer.

The name originates from the bench used in the front of many early 19th-century churches for the church elders or deacons to rest upon during the service.

Most of the benches were used in homes, on porches, or in front

Plate 16. Maple chopping block.

TEXT CONTINUED ON PAGE FORTY-FOUR

Plate 17. Sycamore chopping block.

Plate 18. Meat block, early 20th century.

of stores and public buildings. Many were factory-made by eastern chair manufacturers. They were made with little fundamental change in style throughout the 19th century. They are found today in sizes ranging from five to twelve feet in length. The buyer should realize that many of the larger benches have been cut in half to make two smaller ones. An arm is added to each half and it is usually quite difficult to notice the alterations.

Chopping Blocks

The chopping block illustrated in Plate 16 serves as an excellent end table. It has a diameter of twenty-three inches and stands twenty-eight inches high. This block was taken as a section from a maple tree. Its diminutive size makes it an especially choice piece of country furniture. The much larger blocks are almost impossible to move and their size limits their adaptability within the home.

The block pictured in Plate 17 was cut down to serve as a coffee table. This circular sycamore block stands sixteen inches off the floor in the country home of Mr. and Mrs. John Curry of Four Oaks, Mahomet, Illinois.

Meat and chopping blocks are found in two distinct forms. Round blocks made from sections of trees and square blocks were commercially made and sold to grocers. Circular blocks are considered to be of an earlier vintage than the more commonly found square or rectangular blocks. Chopping blocks vary considerably in size as evidenced by Plates 16–18. Some weigh as much as six hundred pounds and others can be easily lifted by a single man.

Circular blocks with the legs cut down can be transformed into attractive and indestructable coffee tables. Plate 17 aptly illustrates this point.

Occasionally the buyer will chance upon a block stored in a basement for many years or discarded by a local grocery store. These blocks are probably "dished out" to some extent. A "dished out" block has a top that has been used for cutting almost exclusively on one certain section of it. Thus the top or chopping surface is

Plate 19. Occasional table, circa 1840. This pine and poplar table dates from about 1840. The lamp on the table was made from a stoneware "bird" jug. These jug lamps are very easily made and add to a country setting. Stoneware jugs with figures of animals or birds are uncommon. The pine octagon-shaped schoolhouse clock dates from the late 19th century.

not flat. The buyer may overcome this problem by taking the block to a mill and having two or three inches sliced off the top. The charge should be minimal and the results impressive.

Tables and Washstands

Small country tables or washstands in pine, poplar, or walnut are frequently found in shops and at antiques shows. They normally are covered with several coats of paint and show the typical signs of wear. Refinished small tables should be carefully examined as they are being reproduced.

The four tables illustrated in Plates 19–22 were made within a twenty year period on either side of 1860. They are almost impossible to date accurately because changes in style and construction came very slowly to country craftsman in the 19th century.

One method of approximating the date of a particular piece is to check the method the maker used to put the drawers together. Many drawers are held together by dovetails. A dovetail is a carpentry procedure used to interlock two pieces of wood at a corner. The earliest pieces have a single dovetail holding the drawers together. A hand crafted piece of country furniture should have dovetails differing to some degree in size and possibly in number from drawer to drawer. An example with dovetails that are exactly alike and regularly spaced was probably factory-made after 1870. Furniture factories developed machines that automatically dovetailed drawer fittings in the late 19th century. These factory-stamped dovetails are readily apparent, even to the novice, because of their constant regularity in shape and spacing. The machine, unlike the country craftsman, seldom miscalculated in its work.

The typical country table is of simple design. Pine, poplar, and walnut were commonly used in construction. These tables served varied uses within the homes. Some were made to accommodate the bedroom wash bowl and pitcher. Others held a candleholder or a wooden bowl filled with fruit to ease the guest's digestive tract.

TEXT CONTINUED ON PAGE FIFTY

Plate 20. This is a pine bedside or occasional table dating from about 1870. The milk pitcher is an example of spatterware from the late 19th century. The term "spatter" suggests the manner in which the decoration was applied to the pitcher. The iron miner's candle looks much more ancient than it actually is. The sharp point was driven into the mine wall to light the miner's work area. The light also has a hanging hook on the side. This particular piece of lighting dates from about 1880.

Plate 21. Pine table. This two-drawer table is an exceptional piece of country furniture. Most small tables have only a single drawer. The elaborately turned legs of the table also are unusual. This table dates from the mid-19th century.

Plate 22. Bedside table, circa 1850.

Figure 4. 19th century "meal" bin. Bins of this type were used throughout the nineteenth century and well into the twentieth to store various household and farm supplies. Most were used to store grain. Bins are found in pine and poplar and seldom are elaborately constructed. The example illustrated has a scalloped top board and sides. Bins are being used today as stereo cabinets, bars, blanket chests, dirty clothes hampers, and "early American" garbage cans. A bin with a bottom drawer is especially collectible.

Blanket Chests

Lift top, simply constructed blanket chests were a part of every early 19th-century country home. The example shown in Plate 23 is still being used for its original purpose. Many of the handcrafted blanket chests were heavily decorated by hand or with stenciled designs. If the buyer should happen upon such a chest, or any other piece of stenciled or painted country furniture, he should refrain from refinishing it and destroying the examples of early American folk art it may carry.

Blanket chests are not uncommon and are found primarily in pine or poplar. Historians write that the chest was among man's first forms of furniture. In addition to storing his possessions in it, he could also sit or sleep on it. Blanket chests were a part of every household in the 18th and 19th century because all families had valued linens and quilts that were saved for "company."

The typical country home in the early 19th century seldom contained more than a single chest of drawers. The frontier farmer and small-town American of the period typically had no more than two or three changes of clothing. The families had little use for a chest other than to store the family linen and documents. As the country grew and rural America became more conscious of urban styles and fashions, a need for additional household furnishings

Figure 5. A 19th-century doughbox or dough trough. Most of these boxes were made of pine. Doughboxes without legs are also found occasionally. Note the dovetailed sides of this particular example.

TEXT CONTINUED ON PAGE FIFTY-SIX

Plate 23. Blanket chest, circa 1860. The child's iron stove on top of the pine blanket chest above is intact with the original pots, pan, and skillet that brightened a little girl's day one hundred Christmas's ago. The china doll is of the same period. The iron coffee mill at right is dated 1886 and was made in Philadelphia, Pennsylvania. Mills of this type were used both at home and on counter tops in grocery stores to grind coffee.

Plate 24. Chest of drawers, factory-made, circa 1875.

Plate 25. Open or hutch cupboard, early 19th century, also called a "pewter" cupboard. Cupboards of this type were a valued part of many rural homes in the 18th and early 19th centuries. This particular example is constructed of pine. The stoneware jug at the left is an especially fine example of an early Pennsylvania "bird" jug. The cupboard displays old blue Chelsea china in the peacock pattern. The porcelain figurines are German.

Plate 26. Loop-back Windsor chair, early 19th century.

developed. By this time factories were mass-producing inexpensive furniture that was readily available to rural customers through catalogues or the local general store. The rural citizenery found that it was far easier to order a piece of furniture through the mail readymade than wait for the local craftsman to construct one.

Windsor Chairs

The type of Windsor chair shown in Plate 26 has been made in the United States in various forms since the early 18th century. The chair originated in the area of Windsor, England, a century earlier.

The seat of the country Windsor shown in Plate 26 is made from a two-inch plank of pine. The spindles are made of hickory and the legs of maple. The back of the chair is also made of hickory.

Most Windsor chairs were painted. This was done because they were constructed of several different kinds of wood. Old Windsor chairs are not easily found today. The example shown in Plate 26 was made by a country craftsman. It is a copy of the more formal Windsors that were popular in the urban areas of colonial America. The maker of this chair simplified the formal Windsor in his construction. Fanback and comb-back Windsors are rarely seen today.

Chapter Four

COUNTRY KITCHEN ANTIQUES

THE EIGHTEENTH AND EARLY NINETEENTH-CENTURY kitchen utensils were for the most part hand-crafted. It was not until the years immediately preceding the Civil War that factories began turning out mass-produced kitchen were on a large scale. Prior to this period most utensils needed by the housewife were made by her husband or by a local or traveling craftsman. The number of these hand-crafted kitchen articles found for sale today is rapidly diminishing. This chapter will include examples and descriptions of the early hand-crafted pieces and the later factory-made items.

Woodenware

The people of rural America made use of their woodenware kitchen utensils until they were broken or simply worn out. It usually was much easier to have a new implement made than to repair an old one. These utensils were produced to be used and then discarded.

With the coming of the factory period and mass-produced woodenware and other kitchen articles to the shelves of country stores in the mid-19th century, people found it relatively simpler to purchase a particular item than to attempt to craft or forge it by hand.

Hand-crafted kitchen utensils and factory-made products are easily recognized and differentiated. A kitchen spoon made by a machine illustrates the precision and uniformity of its maker's

Plate 27. Hand-carved wooden spoon and factory-made spoon. The top spoon was hand-crafted and used in the making of maple syrup. The bottom factory-produced spoon dates from the turn of the 20th century and had numerous everyday uses in the kitchen. Spoons of this type are found in large quantities in most shops and are inexpensive. Hand-carved spoons are less common because they were disposed of when cracked or broken. Spoons of this type predate 1860.

skills. This machine-made wooden ware is found in almost every shop and dates from the second half of the 19th century through the first decade of the 20th century. The collector should have no difficulty in finding factory-made potato mashers, butter workers and paddles, spoons, butter molds, and wooden chopping or mixing bowls.

Hand-crafted woodenware is equally distinctive in appearance. Often the marks of the maker's tools are visible on the handle of a spoon or ladle or on the underside of a hand-hewn bowl.

In searching for early wooden kitchen pieces the buyer will find geographical influences having serious affects on the availability of many handmade articles. For example, maple sugar molds and sap buckets are more easily found in northern New England than on the plains of Kansas.

The 17th century American learned that each tree in the forest had different uses for the local 'joiners' or carpenters. Maple became a popular choice for making spoons, bowls, mashers, meat pounders, and mortars and pestles for grinding herbs and spices.

Pine was advantageous for making furniture. Oak originally was used for tables, benches, and later for butter churns. Hickory was utilized in making bands to encircle and bind salt boxes, sugar boxes, and churns.

Early kitchen articles such as noggins, trenchers, and tankards are rarely seen in shops today. A noggin is an octagen-shaped pitcher fashioned from a single block of wood. A tankard is a staved pitcher with a lid, used on holidays and special occasions. Trenchers are circular wooden plates that were hand-turned on primitive lathes. They were an improvement over the earlier tradition of the family dining from a single pot placed in the center of the table. Originally trenchers were shared by two members of the family at each meal.

Noggins and trenchers that do appear in the market place today

TEXT CONTINUED ON PAGE SIXTY-FOUR

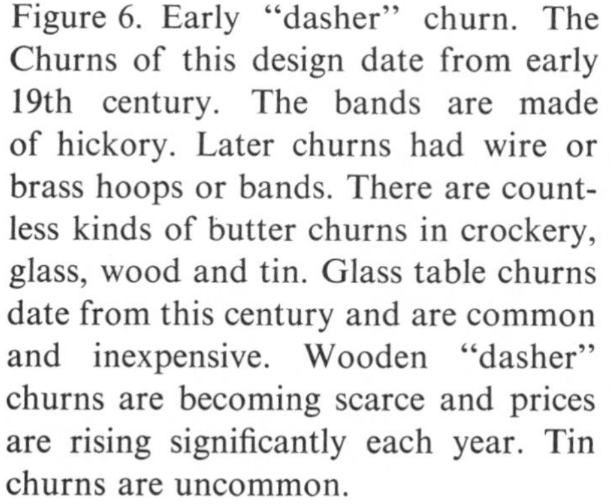

Figure 6. Early "dasher" churn. The Churns of this design date from early 19th century. The bands are made of hickory. Later churns had wire or brass hoops or bands. There are countless kinds of butter churns in crockery, glass, wood and tin. Glass table churns date from this century and are common and inexpensive. Wooden "dasher" churns are becoming scarce and prices are rising significantly each year. Tin churns are uncommon.

Plate 28. Tin strainer, cast iron muffin mold, and unusual grater. The tin strainer above dates from the factory period. The iron muffin mold was used about the same time. Molds of this size are not as common as the larger molds for ten to twelve muffins. Muffin molds are found in a variety of shapes. The pierced-tin food grater on a poplar board dates from the late 18th century. Mary Earle Gould mentions in her definitive *Early American Wooden Ware* that graters of this type were used to scrape carrots. The scrapings were then added to butter to give color.

Plate 29. Wooden spice box, dating from the late 19th century. The boxes were made to be sold quite cheaply. The workmanship and the quality of the materials used in the boxes illustrate this point. Most of the boxes were made to hang on a kitchen wall.

Plate 30. Hanging spice box.

Plate 31. Maple butter molds ranging from a tiny pat to a two-pound size. These factory-made molds date from the 19th century. Molds of this type are also called "beehive" molds. The one at the far right is the earliest of the group.

Plate 32. Butter print or stamp, and uncommon "cow" butter mold. The design on stamps and molds was put into the wood mechanically under great pressure.

should be heavily scarred from many mealtime battles. Tankards were used less frequently and many appear the better for it. Hickory or ash bands were used to bind the staved tankards.

There is a great variety of tin utensils from the factory period (1860–1900) to be found in large quantities in most shops. For the most part these items are fairly inexpensive. The marks of extensive use rather than time often add many years to the appearance of both factory woodenware and tin articles.

This period of machine-made kitchen utensils includes several items that are becoming increasingly scarce and expensive. Every kitchen of a century ago contained a multi-drawered wood or tin hanging chest for spices. Turn-of-the-century mail order catalogues offered the spice boxes for less than a dollar each. The price has multiplied considerably over the years. Spice boxes are found in varying sizes. Most of them contain from six to twelve drawers, with wooden spice boxes being found more frequently than tin. The buyer should try to find a spice box with the lettering ("tea," "cinnamon," "pepper," "mace," "cloves") still on each drawer. It is advisable also to be wary of finding the easily produced reproductions. The drawers of the box should show the effects of its former contents. These may range from faint odors, stains in the bottoms of drawers, or small crystals of salt.

Butter molds and butter stamps are additional factory-produced wooden items that are collected with relish today. Factory-made stamps and molds date from about 1860. Hand-carved stamps predate the factory molds by many years. Butter stamps and molds were used to add a design to butter served at the table. Each family maintained a particular design for many years. Butter molds gave shape to the butter in addition to leaving a decoration. The value of a mold or stamp is largly determined by the design imprinted on it.

The more common ones have simple geometric designs; shocks of wheat, flowers, or acorns. Animal prints are the most sought-after by collectors. A butter print or mold that shows a cow, sheep, rooster, bird, rose, or grasshopper is especially valuable. The American eagle print is among the two or three least commonly

Plate 33. American eagle butter stamp, circa 1860. The eagle is one of the least commonly seen designs on molds and stamps. This example was factory-made of maple. It was painted red with a buttermilk base paint some time during its early days.

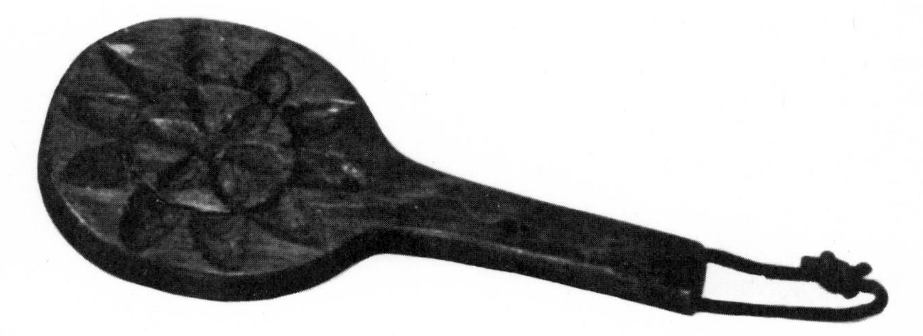

Plate 34. Unusual hand-crafted butter stamp of pine, dating from the early 19th century. Its paddle shape is quite unusual. Most molds and stamps were made of maple wood because of its durability. Pine was seldom used.

Plate 35. Pennsylvania Dutch butter mold with a tulip pattern and "hex" signs. These signs were for decoration rather than a device to drive away the demons. The tulip is one of the more common decorative items on Pennsylvania Dutch pieces. This molds dates from the early 19th century.

seen. The value of this particular print is gradually approaching three figures in many sections of the country. A swan print or mold is the most common animal design found.

The heart-shaped maple-sugar mold in Plate 36 is typical of many used throughout the 19th century. Pine was probably chosen for the mold because of the ease with which it can be worked with a carving knife. Most of the maple sugar harvested in the United States in the 19th century came from northern New York state, Vermont, and New Hampshire. Maple-sugar molds in the shapes of people, birds, farm animals, and geometric designs were used in making candy. Occasionally a rectangular board with several designs on it may be found.

Staved sap buckets with iron bands were made in large quantities and many still survive. The typical sap bucket is painted red or green and is not in good shape.

Plate 36. Hand-carved maple-sugar mold made from a block of pine. Molds of this type were common in New England "sugar" country in the 19th century.

Plate 37. Hand-hewn maple dipper, early 19th century. This dipper is said to have been used as a pickle dipper in a country general store in New Hampshire. It was made from a single piece of wood. Note the holes in the bowl of the dipper. The collector should have little difficulty in acquiring factory-made dippers. They were used in grocery stores well into the 20th century. The dipper above would appear to present a problem for its user when he plunged it into the barrel.

Plate 38. Maple-sugar funnel, circa 1860. This lathe-turned funnel is from upper New York state. It dates from the factory period. Wooden funnels are not common, though funnels of tin and paper-mâché from the same period are. Kitchen funnels of pewter, wood, and copper were made and used in 19th-century country kitchens.

The maple tree, in addition to providing sugar, was used extensively in the production of woodenware and for firewood.

The reader who has an appreciation for or interest in wood is referred to Gould's aforementioned *Early American Wooden Ware* and Eric Sloane's *A Reverence for Wood*. Sloane's informative and informally written book traces the importance of wood in early America. His talent as an author is matched by his ability to illustrate his writing with pen and ink drawings.

Katharine Morrison McClinton's *The Complete Book of American Country Antiques* has an interesting chapter on woodenware with several fine photographs.

The magazines that concern themselves with antiques periodically have articles about early American woodenware. *Spinning Wheel, Antiques Journal,* and *Antiques* are excellent magazines that are becoming increasingly popular as more people become interested in early Americana. Perhaps the best single magazine for collectors of early American antiques is the Maine based *National Antiques Review*.

Country kitchens in the 18th and 19th centuries were stocked with several kinds of wooden bowls. The typical housewife of the period had hand-crafted bowls for cutting and chopping food, and for mixing and rolling dough. Most bowls were made of pine or

TEXT CONTINUED ON PAGE SEVENTY-FOUR

Plate 39. Factory-made kitchen utensils. These are examples of the more commonly found wooden items in most antiques shops. The wooden rolling pin at left and potato masher at right are factory-made of maple. Pieces of this type should not sell for more than a few dollars. They were in use from the mid-19th century well into the 20th century. They are almost impossible to date accurately. The kitchen spoons illustrated are of the same period. The tin piece with the wooden plunger is a cake decorator. It was factory-made in the early 20th century. The butter scoop hanging from the front of the bowl was hand-hewn of pine. It was made for use by a right-handed person. It dates prior to 1850.

Plate 40. Hand-crafted maple dough bowl, circa 1840.

Plate 41. Wooden scoops and confectionary jar, late 19th century. These scoops were made from a single piece of wood. Similar ones were factory-made in the late 19th century. Scoops of this type were used in homes to scoop flour and sugar from bins in kitchen cabinets. They were also used extensively in grocery stores. When found today, the scoops are often cracked and in need of repair. They are not as readily found as scoops made from several pieces of wood. Scoops with the handles nailed on or otherwise attached are not uncommon.

The jar at the left contained sweets from the Candy Brothers Confectioners of St. Louis, Missouri. Jars of this type may be used for a multitude of purposes, including the storing of dried peas.

Plate 42. Early 19th-century kitchen spoon, hand-crafted from a single piece of wood. Mary Earle Gould calls a similar spoon in her collection a "hasty" pudding spoon. The handle is curved to provide leverage when the pudding was taken from the pot. The pudding was made from ground corn and took many hours of stirring.

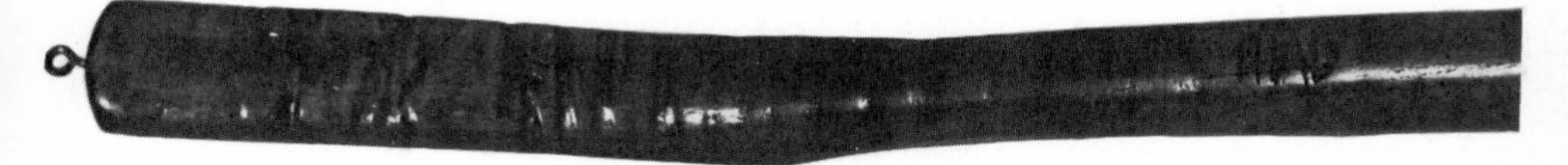

Plate 43. Backside of spoon shown in Plate 42. Note the impressions burned into the handle by the heat of the simmering pot. At the far right the reader may be able to detect the faintly carved name, "Thad." This illustrates one aspect of collecting country antiques that is somewhat unique: the fact that hand-crafted utensils of an early period occasionally give insight into the lives of their makers. It is not too difficult to imagine "Thad" carving his name into the handle of his mother's favorite spoon.

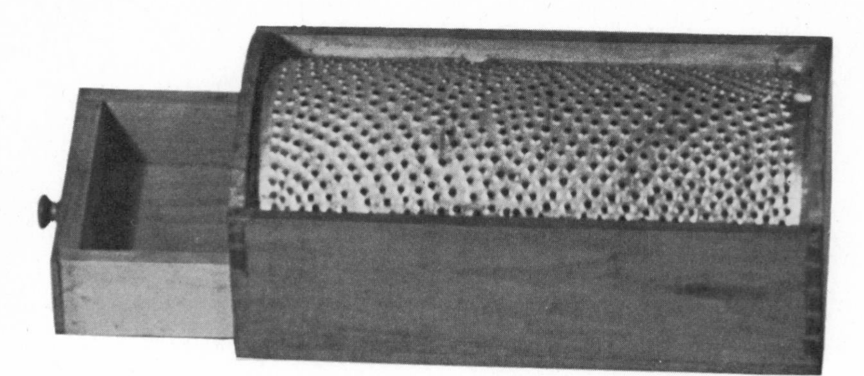

Plate 44. Cheese grater, 19th century, joined at the corners by dovetails.

Plate 45. Wooden hanging salt box, from an 18th-century New England kitchen. It was painted with several coats of a milkbase paint. The beauty of the aged paint is such that it has never been stripped. The bands of the box are hickory. The smaller hole at top right was a knot that has fallen out over the years. Note the unusual decoration at the top. Later salt boxes were made of ironstone. Boxes that were factory-made of wood appeared in the late 19th century.

Plate 46. Unusual initialed knife and fork box, 19th century.

Plate 47. Cookie, candy, and sugar molds, fine examples of early American craftsmanship. The horse and cow carved in pine are maple-sugar candy molds from New England. They date from the early 19th century. The crude heart-shaped mold is probably the earliest of the items shown. It was made about 1800. The three large rectangular molds very possibly are imports. The smaller mold at the far left is for candy. The two larger boards are for molding cookies. The two block letters "C" are from a turn-of-the-century print shop and were used to print large billboard and banner signs.

Plate 48. Pennsylvania spoon rack, circa 1800. This kind of pine rack was used in early 19th century homes for a variety of purposes. The open box on the top contained the householder's long clay pipe. The small drawer below held his tobacco. The shelf holds six spoons on each side of the pipe box. The scalloped bottom ledge was for towels.

maple and were oblong and crudely formed. Circular hand-crafted bowls are seldom seen, though factory-made ones are fairly common. Most of the factory-made bowls were produced after 1860. The mass-produced bowls are almost perfectly formed and show no tool scars as do handmade bowls. The extensive use of these bowls in homes and the passing years have limited their appearance in the market place.

Molds of all types were used in country kitchens of colonial and nineteenth century America. Molds for candles, spoons, buttons, cakes, cookies, maple sugar, puddings, and bullets were common.

Shaker Antiques

In his search for unusual pieces of woodenware, the collector may find a piece with a tag labeled "Shaker," an estimated date and a surprisingly high price. The "Shakers" were a sect of deeply religious people who lived communally in a number of small villages throughout the country. There are several similarities between the Quaker faith and the beliefs of the Shakers. The Shakers were opposed to war and political involvement. Almost any form of entertainment, including sports, instrumental music, and theatrical amusements were prohibited. Possibly the most important manifestation of the faith, to 20th-century antique collectors, are the Shaker household furnishings and utensils.

The Shakers believed in simplicity and a total lack of any "superfluous" decoration. Each Shaker community had written descriptions of "suitable furniture for dwelling rooms." Checkered of flowered rugs or curtains were prohibited and only rugs and curtains of "modest" color were permitted.

Ann Lee, the founder of the Shaker faith, started the first settlement near Albany, New York, in 1776. "Mother" Ann Lee spent much of the remaining eight years of her life traveling throughout New York, Massachusetts, and Connecticut in an attempt to develop more Shaker converts and communities. In later years Shaker communities were started in New England and the Middle West as late as the 20th century.

The number of converts to the Shaker or the United Society of Believers in Christ's Second Appearing, as it was more formally known, peaked during the Civil War with about 6500 members. By 1900 the number had dropped to about 1000. Scholars suggest the decline in membership was due to a relaxation of the former rigid rules that governed the Shaker's daily life. Shaker furniture of the late 19th century began to take on a slight Victorian appearance.

TEXT CONTINUED ON PAGE EIGHTY

Plate 49. Shaker butter churn, circa 1840. This is an excellent example of the type of work the Shakers did in the late 18th and 19th centuries. Note especially the "lapping" holding the staves together.

Plate 50. Late 19th-century coffee mills of tin and wood, and three additional examples of "dasher" butter churns. The center churn is of the earliest vintage, dating from the early 19th century. Note the bands encircling each churn. Those on the one at the left are made of wire. The factory-made churn at right has brass bands and dates from the late 19th century.

Plate 51. Cottage cheese molds of varying sizes, 19th century.

Plate 52. Hand-crafted pine bowl and apothecary jars, 19th century.

Plate 53. Hanging kitchen box, early 19th century. This kind of pine hanging box had various uses in early nineteenth-century kitchens. It may have been used for candles, spoons, knives, or as a general utility box. Like country antiques, it is imperfectly constructed. Note how the bottom level slants significantly to the left. The maker also was not frugal with nails as attested by the sixteen in the upper area alone. The open bowls below include a staved cottage cheese mold, a hand-hewn pine chopping bowl, and a pinewood sheep "lick" that held salt.

Plate 54. Early wooden boxe, and bowls.

The early Shakers were poor people with little financial backing to start their communities. It is for this reason they began to provide for themselves and develop their own woodworkers and craftsmen. The religious goal of freedom from needless ornamentation and material goods had a great effect on the Shaker craftsmen and their products. The Shaker workers turned away from the "adultery" of more worldly cabinetmakers who added to the appearance of their works with carved legs and drawer pulls. Eventually the laws of the faith concerning design were such that there was a great uniformity in the furniture turned out in the various communities, even to the types of paint and stains used.

The Shakers combined their skill as farmers with the ability to turn out furniture, woodenware, tools, clocks, baskets, and boxes that were sold to their more worldly neighbors. The pieces of Shaker construction that the collector happens upon in his travels have probably been passed down through the family of a customer of the Shakers.

The Shaker Museum in Old Chatham, New York serves as a depository today for a great many examples of the Shaker craft.

Coffee grinders or mills of the type shown in Plate 50 were used in homes of the late 19th and early 20th centuries. The mill at left was made in Europe. The simpler wooden one at the right was manufactured in the United States. Inexpensive mills are commonly found in most antiques shops. Coffee bean roasters are much less common than coffee mills. Some coffee bean roasters resemble simple popcorn poppers. The circular roasters with handles were often placed on the top of a wood-burning stove.

Articles in copper and brass, ranging from teapots to bed warmers, are still found in most antique shops. Kitchen utensils of copper and brass are common. The brass skimmer in Plate 56 was found in southern Pennsylvania. It has an iron handle and copper rivets holding it together.

The best examples of early American and English teakettles should have "dovetailed" bottoms and gooseneck pouring spouts. The kettles were products of colonial America and England in the

TEXT CONTINUED ON PAGE EIGHTY-EIGHT

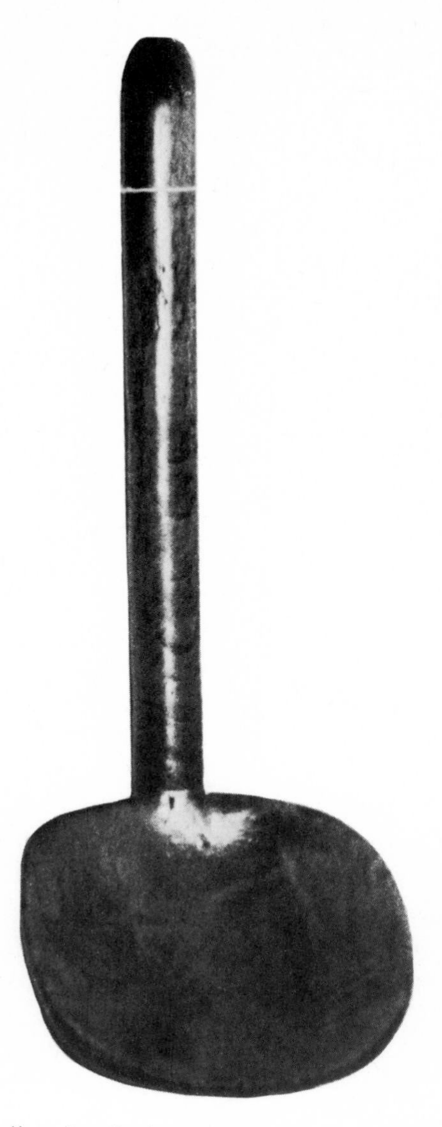

Plate 55. Butter "worker," circa 1840. These were used to press the water out of freshly churned butter. After the butter was removed from the churn it was "worked." This one was hand-crafted. Later, machine-made "workers" are found in large quantities in most shops.

Plate 56. Brass skimmer. Plate 57. Iron spatula. Plate 58. Copper ladle. The three items shown in Plates 56–58 all date from the mid-19th century.

Plate 59. Copper apple-butter kettle with iron bale handle, 19th century.

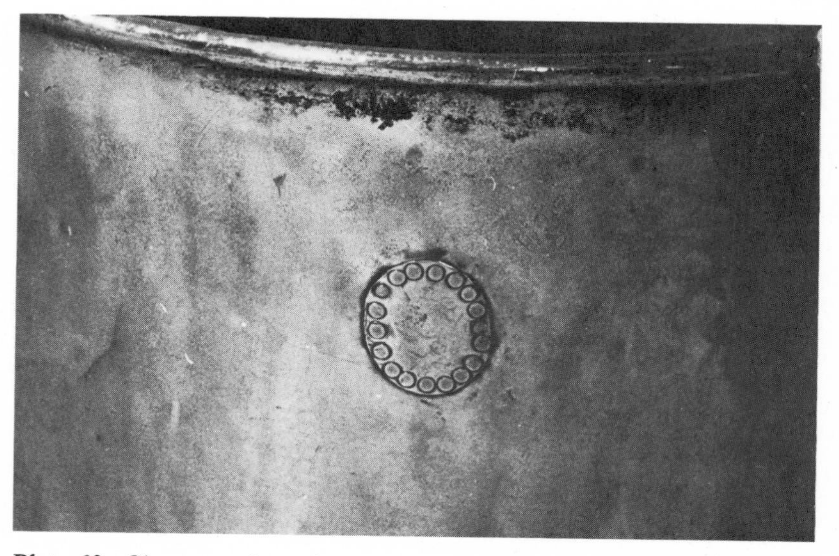

Plate 60. Close-up of repairs made to the apple butter kettle shown in Plate 59.

Plate 61. Copper teakettle with gooseneck spout, circa 1820.

Plate 62. Copper teakettle, 19th century.

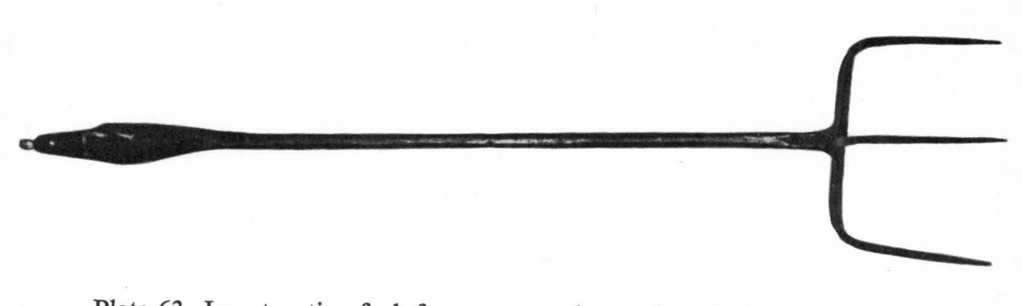

Plate 63. Iron toasting fork for use around open hearth, 19th century.

Plate 64. Copper cooking pots, American southwest, late 19th century, typical of many that are still available. The two smaller pots at left are bean pots. These were used on the range by cattlemen to heat their evening meal over a fire. A stake was put through the two handles as shown in Figure 7 to suspend the pot. The larger pot was factory-made and served a variety of purposes. These date from about 1880.
Figure 7. Copper bean pot.

Plate 65. Tole (tin) milk can, pitcher-measure, and cream can, circa 1870.

Plate 66. Ironstone rolling pin, pie crimpers, egg beater, and cheese board, circa 1890.

Plate 67. Chopping knife, tin and copper gelatine mold, large gelatine or pudding mold, and, most interesting of all, a Pennsylvania Dutch doughnut cutter. This tin cutter produced holeless doughnuts ready for deep-fat frying.

Plate 68. Iron scale, possibly used in drug store, late 19th century.

Plates 69 & 70. Unusual wheeled iron spice grinder, used in a late 19th-century home. The grinder stands nine inches high. In addition to being ground in devices like the one illustrated, spices were purchased in general stores and hand-ground with a mortar and pestle.

18th and early 19th centuries. Late 19th- and early 20th-century kettles are quite simple; they are likely to be covered with nickel and bear the manufacturer's mark.

The copper piece illustrated in Plate 59 is an apple butter kettle. Apple butter was a popular garnish for food and baked goods in early America. The apple butter was made in kettles, heated, and constantly stirred over a fire. Apple butter kettles are found in a variety of sizes. The typical kettle had a wrought iron bail handle and rested in a three-legged iron stand over the fire. Large wooden apple butter stirrers are also occasionally found. A stirrer resembles a "foot" on a long broomlike handle. The "foot" has holes in it to allow the butter to pass through while being stirred. The kettle illustrated in Plate 59 points out the innate thrift of the 19th century

TEXT CONTINUED ON PAGE NINETY-FOUR

Plate 71. Hand-forged iron trivet, 18th century, used in front of an open hearth to keep meals warm until served.

Iron trivets were also made for toasting bread. The handle on the example above has a hole in it for hanging on the wall or fireplace beam when not in use. Trivets are fairly expensive examples of colonial workmanship.

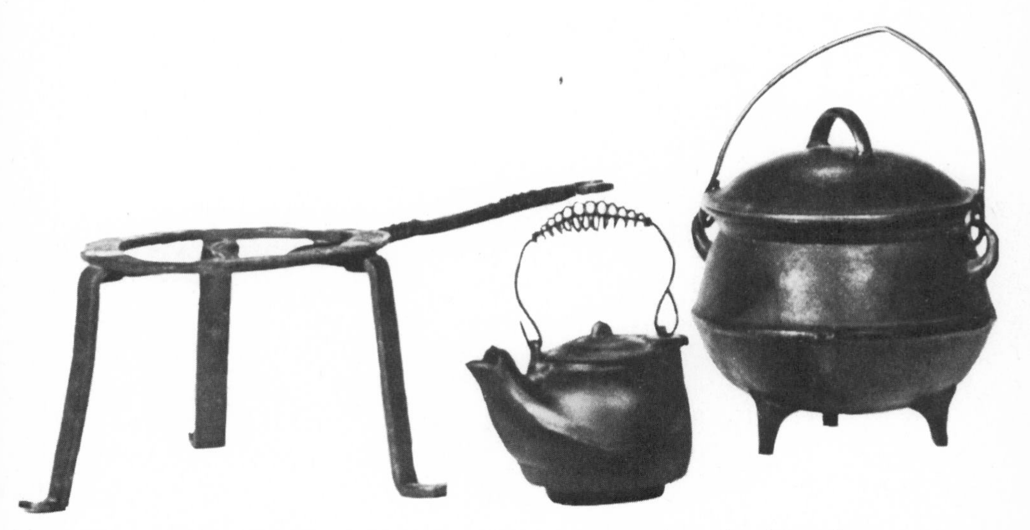

Plate 72. 18th-century iron trivet, salesman's sample teakettle, and an iron pot.

Plate 73. Crockery salt and butter containers, circa 1900.

Plate 74. Stoneware jar and wire basket used to gather eggs.

Plate 75. Iron cooking pot.

Plate 76. Child's unique teakettle on tiny trivet and salesman's sample kettle. Every salesman who traveled the countryside with his wares was faced with a similar problem: How to transport his merchandise? Many companies solved the problem by making miniatures of their products. Thus the seller of meat blocks carried tiny blocks to show his customers. The tea kettle peddler carried kettles similar to the one above.

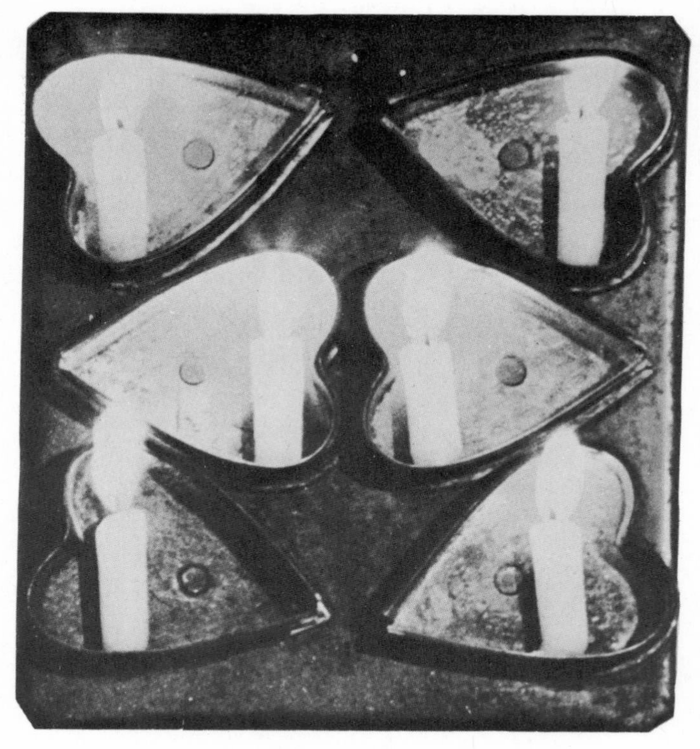

Plate 77. Tin sugar mold.

Plate 78. Blending of country antiques with Ethan Allen desk, showing how easy it is to use small antiques to accentuate newly-made early American furniture. Many people furnish their homes with high quality furniture from local stores, and after expending a large sum of money, realize that they have cultivated an unfulfilled taste for authentic early American antiques. It is difficult to understand why one who enjoys country furniture does not initially furnish his home with the "real" thing, rather than with more expensive reproductions. It is possible, however, to decorate a home furnished with newly made early American furniture by collecting smaller items in wood, crockery, iron, and tin from an earlier period. Displayed on the Ethan Allen desk, above, are several examples of early lighting, an eight-drawer spice chest, a heart-shaped maple sugar mold, and a small spice grinder. See page 93.

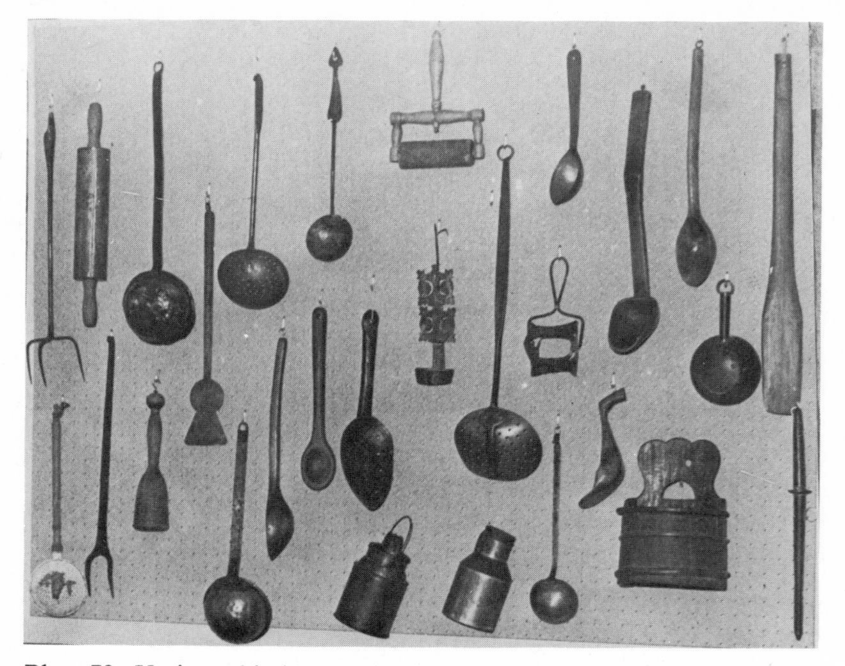

Plate 79. Various kitchen antiques. Here are examples of country kitchen antiques, some of which are illustrated individually on other pages. The rolling pin is made of tin but with the standard wooden handles. The two-prong iron toasting fork at the lower left was hand-forged in the early nineteenth century. The wooden spoons are all hand-crafted as is the iron spoon at the left of the hasty pudding spoon.

American. The owner of the kettle took special pains to have it repaired. The copper patch is held in place by brass rivets. This kettle and the tea kettle in Plate 61 have both been professionally sealed and burnished.

Burnishing keeps an article from tarnishing over the years. This apple butter kettle was covered with a thick black coating of carbon from countless fires when the authors purchased it. Several hours of work failed to make any impression on the carbon covering, so the kettle was turned over to a professional for cleaning.

Many collectors refrain from having their purchases in copper and brass professionally cleaned. They feel that the many years of use and abuse have left a "look" that should be maintained.

Plates 64 through 68 show a number of kitchen pieces that are not uncommon in shops today. The copper bean pots in Plate 64 are found in several sizes. Copper cooking pots were and are the first choice of chefs.

The tin or tole factory-made milk cans in plate 65 are interesting. The milk can with the wood stopper was used by a child when he toted his lunch to school. The tin kitchen utensils found in shops today usually are factory-made, inexpensive, and quite abundant.

Many grocery stores that opened their doors in the late 19th and early 20th centuries distributed ironstone rolling pins to their customers. The most commonly found rolling pins are of maple, though tin pins are occasionally seen. Pie crimpers or jiggers were used to cut the crust in a decorative fashion prior to baking. Crimpers were made of ironstone, tin pewter, and whale bone.

Fig. 7. Copper bean pot.

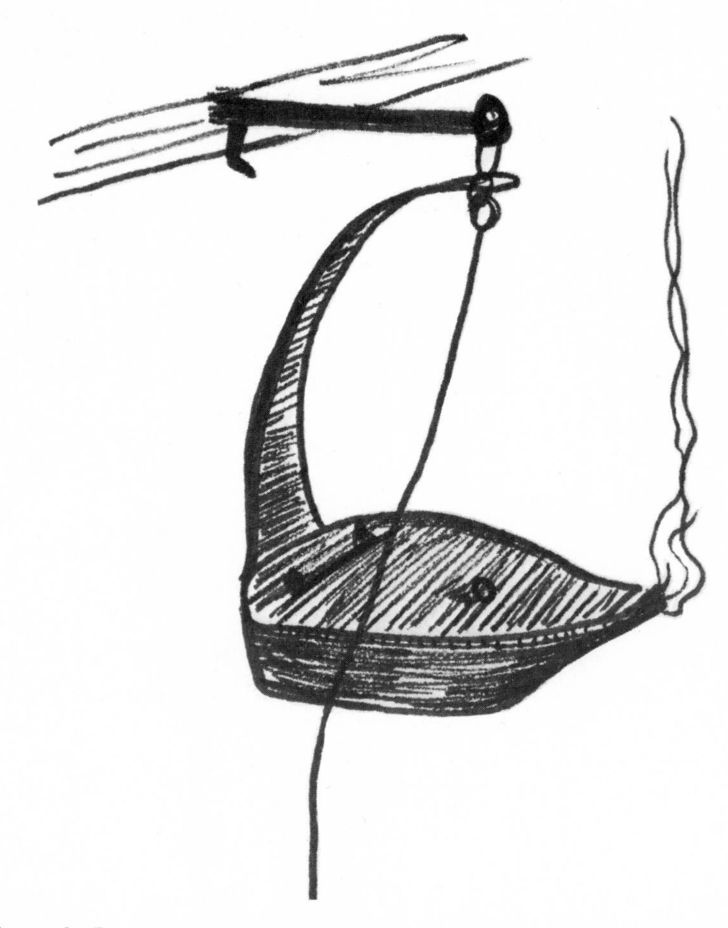

Figure 8. Iron betty lamp, 18th century. Such lamps provided but meager light for many frontier homes in the 18th and early 19th centuries. They were made of iron, tin, brass, copper, and earthenware. Some pewter lamps were made but are extremely rare today. Iron and tin betties are still found in large quantities.

Chapter Five

EARLY ARTIFICIAL LIGHTING

UNLIKE MANY ASPECTS of life in colonial America, artificial lighting underwent relatively little alteration from the settling of Plymouth Colony to the middle of the 19th century.

Undoubtedly among the first forms of artificial lighting used by our Pilgrim fathers were the iron "betty" and crusie lamps. The origin of the term "betty" is far from certain. Some writers feel the name stems from the early English word "bettyngs," meaning oil or fat. It is also suspected that the name came from the German "besser" meaning "better." Other researchers suggest the French "petit," meaning small or tiny.

The "betty" and the crusie differ little from the grease- and oil-burning lamps used three thousand years before the first white man stumbled on North America. Earthenware grease lamps found in diggings in ancient Greece and Egypt differ little from those brought to the New World by the English immigrants. Prior to 1700 only a minimal change had occurred in artificial lighting in more than 3500 years. The grease- or fat-burning lamp was as well known in ancient Athens as it was in the Plymouth Colony.

A "betty" lamp consists of a shallow grease-filled metal dish or cup with a support to hold the burning wick upright. The wick normally was a piece of twisted linen rag. The metal dish, which was fashioned from a single piece of iron, was connected to a pick by a wrought-iron chain two or three inches long. The pick was used for pulling the wick out of the dish to make it burn more brightly. The lamps were hung by an iron spindle with a hooked end. The hooked end was used to hang the lamp from a chair or suspend it from a loose stone over the hearth.

A crusie is a pear-shaped, open-pan type lamp with a spout for the wick to lie in. The pan is usually about an inch deep. A crusie with a second open pan directly below the first is called a double crusie or a "Phoebe" lamp. The second pan is attached to catch the drippings of the upper pan.

The "betty" lamp differs from the crusie in that it has a cover and a half-round wick support on the pan to hold it in place. The wick support is located in the middle of the pan. A "betty" also has a less crude and primitive appearance than the typical crusie.

The collector may still find examples of "betty" lamps, crusies and double crusies ("Phoebes"), for sale in shops that specialize in fine country antiques. The buyer should be sure to check the lamp carefully before purchasing it to make sure it is intact. Often the pick is missing or the chain has been replaced. Most of the lamps found today date from the late 18th century through the mid-19th century.

These lamps are capable of burning several types of fuel including fish oil, animal fat, and 20th-century Crisco. The oil from fish livers initially was used because of its availability. The unpleasant odor and the small amount of light produced led the people of the period to search for a more agreeable fluid. Beef fat, deer fat, and oil from the sperm whale were also used.

Fishing for whales in small open boats near the New England shoreline became a growing industry in the late 17th century. The oil from sperm whales proved to be vastly superior to any kind formerly used. The amount of light produced by whale oil was greater than that of animal fat, and the odor was appreciatively diminished.

Rush lights provided a primitive source of illummation in New England during the 17th and 18th centuries. They were used by the first settlers in place of candles. The light was provided by pith taken from reeds that grew in abundance in surrounding swamp areas. The pith was dipped in tallow or animal fat and then placed in an iron holder. The rushes were held in place by iron tongs or

Plate 80. Iron double crusie.

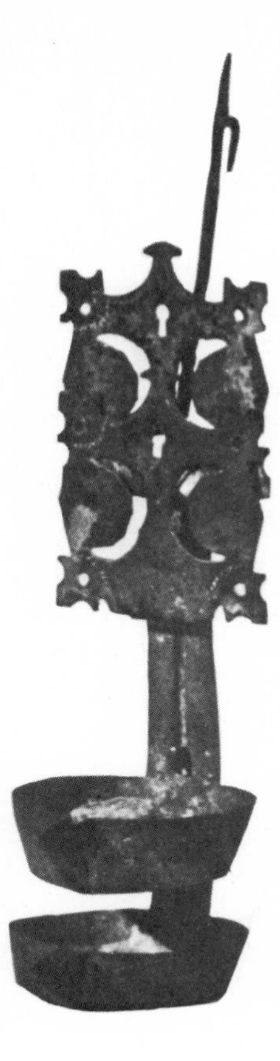

Plate 81. Tin candle sconce, circa 1825. This is an excellent example of early American artificial lighting. A sconce is a lighting device in which a light source is placed in front of a reflector that also protects the light from draft. The typical sconce had a candle as the light source. Some candle sconces have a glass reflector.

Figure 9. Punched-tin candle lantern dating from early 19th century. Some rare lanterns have carefully scraped cow horns rather than more common glass panels surrounding the candle.

Figure 10. Iron rush light holder, dating from about 1700. Lighting enthusiasts may still happen upon a rush light in shops that stock items for the advanced collector. Many examples have a crude hardwood base.

Figure 11. "Paul Revere" pierced-tin candle lantern, the kind that supposedly graced the tower of the Old North Church in Boston. Lanterns of this type actually cast very little light.

pinchers. The rush light holder shown in Figure 10 also has a socket attached to hold a candle.

Another method of artificial lighting that was used for over one hundred and fifty years was produced by tallow or wax candles. Cattle were brought to the expanding colonies about the middle of

TEXT CONTINUED ON PAGE ONE HUNDRED FOUR

Plate 82. Rare twelve-tube circular candle mold.

Plate 83. Uncommon smaller candle molds in tin, early 19th century. The molds at the far left and right were hung on a wall while the candles were being formed in the tubes. Most of the molds that are found are constructed of tin. Earthenware and copper candle molds are quite rare.

Plate 84. Twelve-tube copper candle mold and a hanging six-tube mold.

Plate 85. Forty-eight tube chandler's mold.

Plate 86. Thirty-six tube tin mold.

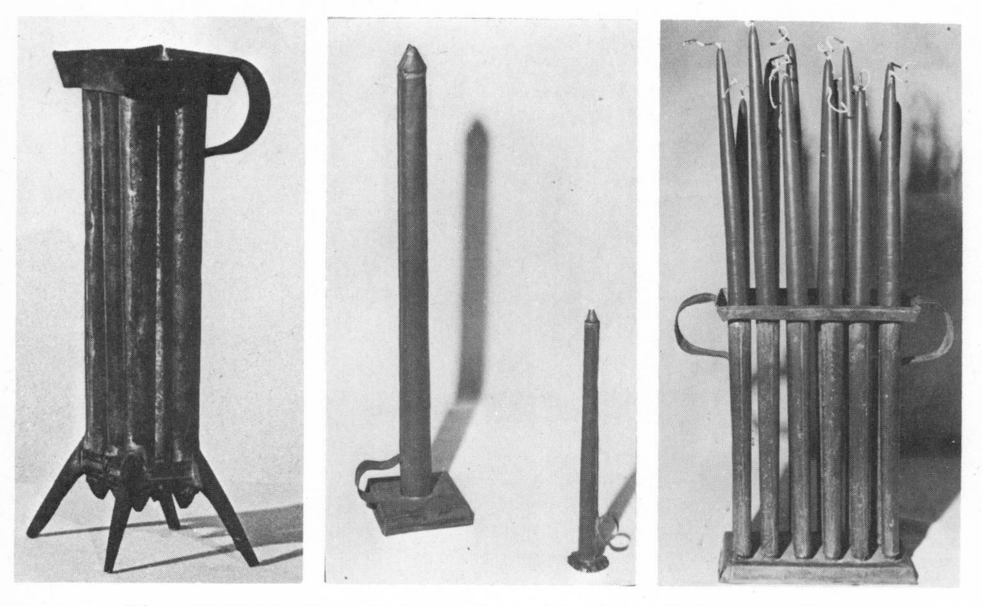

Plate 87 (*left*). Footed tin candle mold. Plate 88 (*center*). Single-tube candle molds. The one at the left, which stands 19″ tall, was used to make altar candles in a 19th-century church. The smaller mold at right, which has a fluted base, was found in eastern Pennsylvania. Both are of the hanging variety. Candle molds with one, two, or three tubes are uncommon. Small molds were used by housewives in making their candles. Plate 89 (*right*). Eighteen-tube tin candle mold.

the 17th century. Prior to the arrival of cattle, candles were made from the fat of wild animals found in large numbers in nearby woods.

Candles were also made from wax found in the honey combs of bees, from the berry of the bayberry bush, and from spermaceti. Spermaceti is a fatty substance found in the head cavities of sperm whales.

Spermaceti candles were considered next to bayberry or "candle-berry" candles in desireability. Spermaceti candles give off an excellent light with little smoke. Bayberry candles also provide much light with a small amount of smoke, and emit a fragrant odor when

Plate 90. Tin candle box, circa 1800, the kind that was made and sold by traveling tinsmiths in the early 19th century to store candles that had a tendency to yellow when exposed to the air after being made. This candle box was made to hang on a wall.

extinguished. Bayberry bushes are found along the coast of the Atlantic Ocean. The berries were in such demand in 17th century New England that laws were passed limiting the season during which they could be picked.

Candles were made in two distinct different ways. They were either dipped by hand or molded in tin candlemolds. Dipping was a lengthy process in which the amount of tallow was gradually built up on a wick after repeating the dipping process countless times. Dipping required little skill but much patience. The chief problem in dipping candles was to keep the tallow at such a temperature that when dipped it would not melt the tallow already adhering to the wick. The dipping usually took place in the fall during slaughtering time. The cattle were butchered to supply the winter's meat and the fat was used to make candles. It was possible for a housewife to dip as many as two hundred candles in a long work day.

TEXT CONTINUED ON PAGE ONE HUNDRED TEN

Plate 91. Punched-tin candle lantern, 19th century, of the "Paul Revere" type. These lanterns have been and currently are being mass-produced in large quantities. It is possible to treat them with acid or bury them in moist soil in such a way that even lighting authorities have difficulty in dating them. Reproductions tend to run about twenty to forty dollars in price. Genuine old lanterns should have the appearance of being hand-punched rather than machine-stamped.

Plate 92. Wood-framed candle lantern, circa 1830, made of walnut wood with a tin top. Wood-framed lanterns are less common than tin or iron candle lanterns. The lamp (s) that hung in the Old North Church is thought to be more of this type than the previously described "Paul Revere" lantern. The glass panels that collectors find in lamps of this type should have bubbles and wavy lines in it. When looked through at an angle, the image should be slightly distorted.

Plate 93. Candle lantern and tin skater's lantern.

Plate 94. Brass candle lantern, English, 19th century.

Plate 95. Kerosene lanterns dating from about 1862 to 1900. The tin kerosene lamp at left has a patent date of 1860. It is from the extensive lighting collection of Mr. and Mrs. Elmer Fedder of Winchester, Illinois. The lamp at far right is shown courtesy of Mr. and Mrs. Charles Faulkner of Dupo, Illinois.

Plate 96. Three whale oil lamps dating from about 1850.

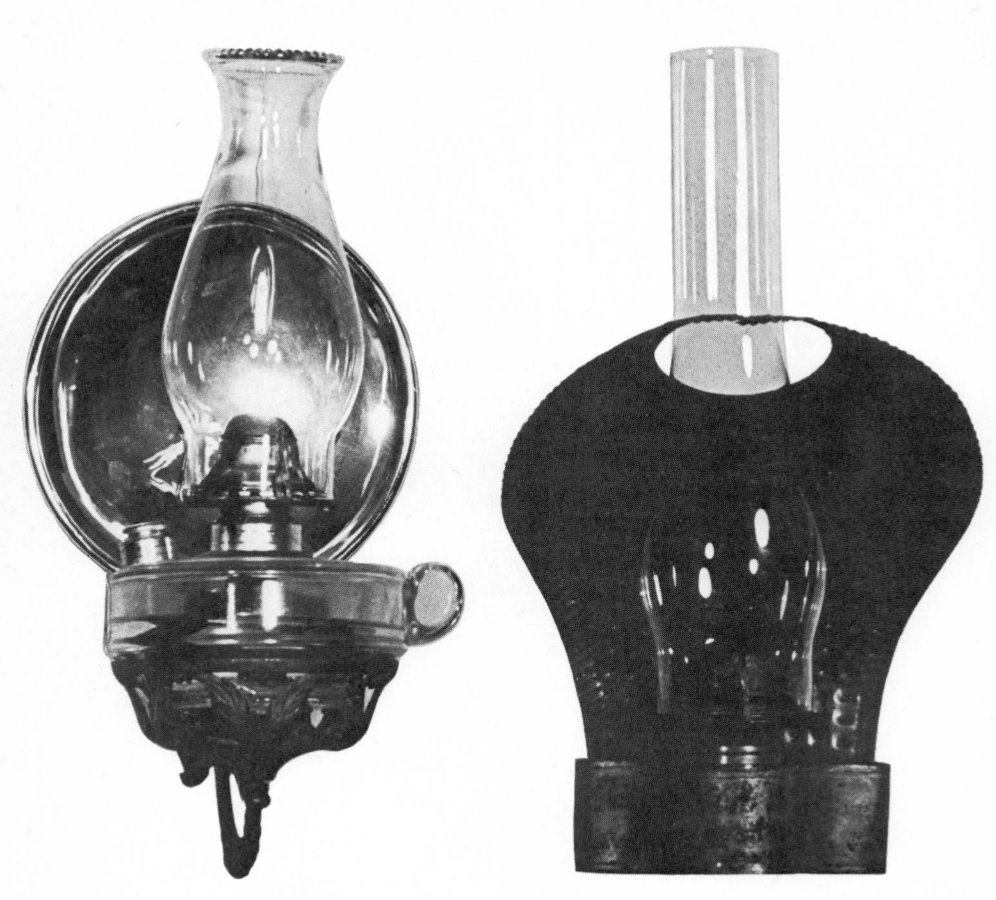

Plate 97 (*left*). Kerosene lamp used in railway car, circa 1880.

Plate 98 (*right*). Glass kerosene lamp in iron holder with mercury reflector. These are now being reproduced in large quantities. The one shown above dates from the late 19th century. Note the circular glass finger hole on the right of the lamp. This was used when the lamp was removed from the holder and held. The mercury reflector was a great improvement over the earlier tin reflector shown in Plate 79.

Candle molds are a development of colonial America, though the actual invention is credited to a Frenchman. Candle molds in reasonably good condition are becoming increasingly difficult to find. The molds that do appear in the market place usually contain four, six, eight, or twelve tubes. Most molds have the tubes arranged in a rectangular fashion. Footed molds, molds with the tubes arranged in a circular manner, and molds with an odd number of tubes are rarely found.

Candle molds that contained as many as twelve dozen tubes were made by tinsmiths. These were used by chandlers, who were traveling candlemakers and salesmen, and who were known in every outlying hamlet. The chandlers were popular sources of communication between villages and farms in an age when newspapers were few and even farther between.

Whale oil lamps were popular during the first half of the 19th century. Between 1800 and 1845 more than five hundred patents for whale oil lamps were granted to inventors in the United States.

Kerosene or coal oil lamps came into use after the Civil War and are still being used on occasion today. Common glass kerosene lamps are found in large quantities in most shops at reasonable prices.

Figure 12. Earthenware grease lamp.

The earlier whale oil lamps are fairly rare and costly examples of early artificial lighting. There are countless varieties of whale oil lamps, most being made from tin. Some were also made of glass or brass, and occasionally of pewter. Whale oil lamps were replaced by the kerosene or coal oil lamps when oil became readily available. Leroy Thwing in his excellent book, *Flickering Flames,* calls the kerosene lamp the ". . . best oil-burning lighting device the world has ever known."

The illustration of the pottery grease lamp in Figure 12 depicts a form of lighting that is rarely seen. Lamps of this type go back literally thousands of years. The fragility of the lamps is the primary factor in their scarcity. Pottery lamps were made in the United States until about 1850.

Figure 13. Tin whale oil lamp.

Chapter Six

POTPOURRI

THERE ARE MANY KINDS of country antiques that are difficult to classify under such headings as furniture, country kitchen antiques, lighting, and country store items. This chapter contains items that range from samplers and early nineteenth century birth certificates to wooden hay forks and chamber pots.

Wooden shovels and scoops were used throughout the 18th and 19th centuries on farms. They were handmade by the farmers themselves during the long winter months. A farmer who had special skills with a whittling knife could take orders for such wooden tools.

Plate 99. Tin plaque of Lincoln. As was the case following the tragic death of President Kennedy, there were pictures, books, stories, and busts of Lincoln marketed after his assasination. The tin plaque above was found in a rural grocery store where it had been stored for ninety years.

Plate 100. Cast iron bust of Lincoln as a young man, said to have been taken from the McLean County Court House in Bloomington, Illinois that was destroyed by fire in 1900. Lincoln's funeral train passed through Bloomington on its way to Springfield. Lincoln was a familiar face in Bloomington during his career as a lawyer. He gave his famous "Lost Speech" in this central Illinois community.

Plate 101. Pine wood Seth Thomas clock.

Plate 102. Pitcher and bowl, mug, and chamber pot.

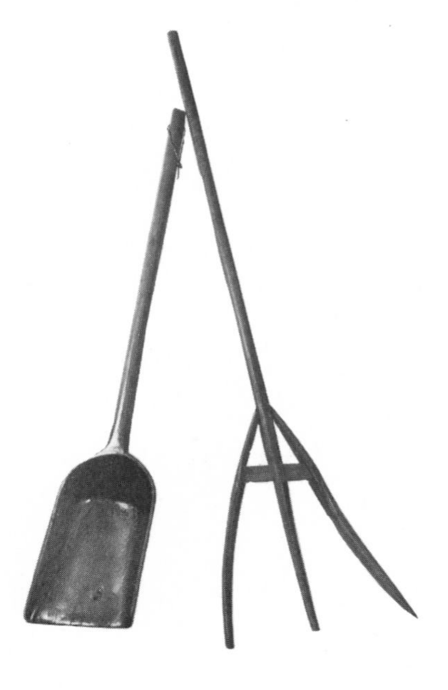

Plate 103. Wooden grain scoop and hay fork. Such items are very popular among collectors of country antiques. They are becoming so popular in fact, that they are being reproduced by many descendants of the original farmer-craftsmen. The reproductions are almost as expensive as originals. Forks and shovels were made from hard woods that could withstand much abuse. In the later part of the 19th century some hay forks were factory-made.

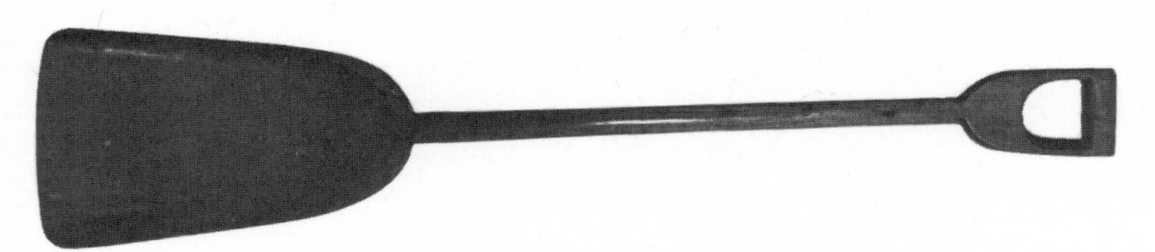

Plate 104. Wooden shovel.

Plate 105. Birth certificate of Angelina Conner, 1842, "slod" by Blummer and Bush of Allentown, Pennsylvania. Angelina was baptized by Reverend D. S. Tobias in Orange County, Columbia Township, Pennsylvania. The American eagle at the top of the certificate and the birds at the bottom left and right are common to many Pennsylvania documents.

Plate 106. Sampler of Harriot Rowbotham, 1829. Samplers were made by young girls throughout the 18th century and into the 19th, until about 1870. A typical sampler includes numbers, the alphabet, the maker's name, a brief prayer, and the date. It is strange that few samplers appear with a date after 1870. Perhaps the coming of mass-produced clothing in large quantities in the late nineteenth century doomed the homemaker's need for skill with needle and thread. The sampler above contains the following brief prayer: "Remember now Thy Creator in Youth." It is from the extensive collection of Mrs. D. J. Raycraft of Normal, Illinois.

Chapter Seven

COUNTRY STORE ANTIQUES

THE GOLDEN AGE of the rural or small town country store stretched from the late nineteenth century through the early twentieth century. Items from these stores that are seriously collected today range from spool and dye cabinets to wheeled coffee grinders, advertising tins and containers, signs, scoops, scales, and chopping blocks.

The country store today connotes a vision of checker boards and pot-bellied stoves in an era when life was seemingly uncomplicated and crackers and pickles were marketed in barrels.

Lavishly decorated iron-wheeled coffee grinders are found in sizes ranging from slightly over twelve inches in height to mammoth grinders on ornate cast iron legs that tower well over five feet. Many of these iron coffee grinders or mills were made by the Enterprise Manufacturing Company of Philadelphia, Pennsylvania. Most of them date from the last thirty years of the 19th century. Often the patent date will appear on the side of one of the wheels. The wheeled coffee grinders that are the most valuable still have the original paint and stenciling. The owner should refrain from repainting a grinder that still carries most of its original decoration.

The buyer of country store coffee grinders should not confuse a wheeled coffee grinder with the more common grain grinder. A grain grinder often has only a single wheel and doesn't have a box for the depositing of its grindings.

Large-wheeled coffee grinders were displayed on the counters of every grocery store in the late 19th century and were used to grind

Plate 107. Enterprise coffee grinder, 19th century. This one is twenty-one and a half inches high and weighs fifty-six pounds. It is finished in red and blue with gold striping. It is capable of grinding a pound of coffee with fifty turns of the wheel. This mill had a catalogue price of $3.50.

coffee beans for the customers. Miniature grinders, usually having a single wheel, were used for grinding spices.

Cabinets that contained packages of dye and spools of thread are found in a variety of sizes. Some spool cabinets are large enough to serve as end tables, others have lift tops and can be used as writing desks. Most of the spool and dye cabinets still being discovered in shops are made of oak. Many have been stained to take on a darker appearance. Dye cabinets usually have the manu-

TEXT CONTINUED ON PAGE ONE HUNDRED TWENTY-TWO

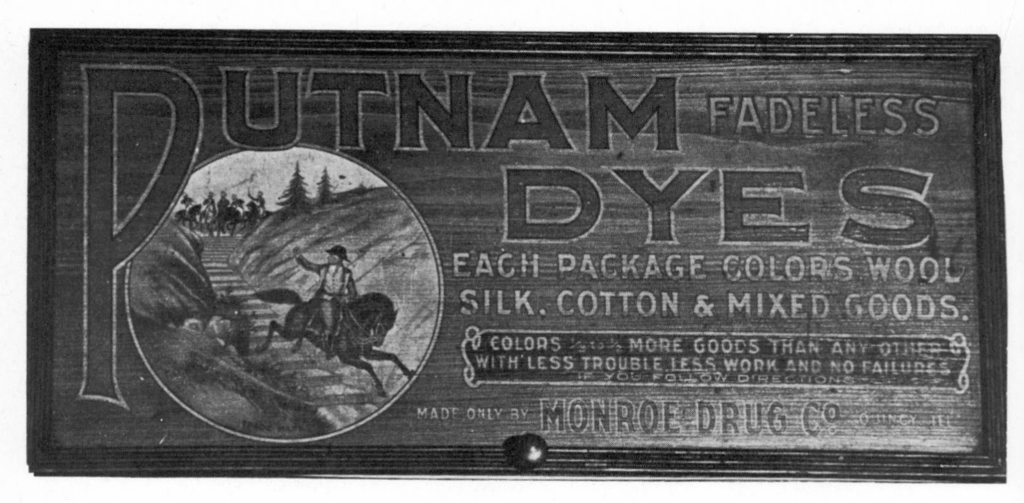

Plate 108. Putnam Dye cabinet with illustration of fleeing Revolutionary soldier.

Plate 109. Early 20th-century containers made of tin, paper, and glass.

Plate 110. Unsigned stoneware jar with cobalt blue flower decoration, filled with bittersweet. It dates from about 1870.

Plate 111. Mid-19th century stoneware crock and jug. Both of these pieces were made by the Hamilton and Jones Pottery of Greensboro, Pennsylvania. The lettering was stenciled on in cobalt blue.

facturer's name and a multi-colored illustration on the front of the door. The Putnam Dye cabinet illustrated in Plate 108 contains a picture of a fleeing General Putnam on horseback being pursued by a host of potential captors in red coats. It dates from the turn of the 20th century.

Tin containers and advertising signs for sale in shops today date from the 1880's through World War I. Tin flour, sugar, baking soda, and tobacco containers are colorful and offer countless decorative possibilities.

The origin of the country store in many rural areas is cloudy. A reasonable explanation for their existence is the tale told of the elderly wandering peddlers who grew tired of covering the countryside and took up permanent residence in the villages and opened up stores to sell their wares.

Plate 112. Stoneware doughnut jar with hand-applied birds.

Plate 113. Stoneware cookie jar, circa 1860.

Plate 114. Two-gallon jug with hand-painted bird.

An advertisement from the early 1800's shows the various articles carried by the typical store: broad cloth, flannels, laces, ribbons, ostrich feathers, coat buttoms, hardware, glass, rum, brown and lump sugar, raisins, spice, pepper, tea, and chocolate. Countless additional items were found on the shelves.

Many of the stores had the policy of exchanging their goods for

Plate 115. Stoneware cooler, dating from the 20th century. Crocks, jugs, and water coolers of this period are abundant and inexpensive.

Plate 116. The Norton Bennington signature. This pottery's first stoneware products were turned out about 1800. In later years they produced a wide variety of wares including door knobs, candlesticks, and wash boards.

the produce and seed grown by local farmers. The stores additionally served as the local post office and dispensary for the bartering of choice bits of local gossip and scandal.

Until the 1870's when paper bags became available in grocery stores, the customers often were obliged to bring their own containers to carry home their purchases.

Plate 117 (*next page*). Four-gallon Bennington stoneware jug made by the E. and L. P. Norton pottery of Bennington, Vermont between 1860 and 1880. The date can be attributed to this period because of the signature pressed into the jug, inasmuch as this was their established practice during that twenty year period. Products of this Bennington, Vermont pottery are probably the most sought-after of any individual pottery in the world. It was established in 1793 and specialized in the making of earthenware household utensils.

E & L P NORTON
BENNINGTON VT.

Plate 118. Needle cabinet. This box dates from the late 19th century. It was made of oak and is presently being used to hold silverware.

For almost one hundred years earthenware or stoneware crockery in all shapes and sizes was found abundantly in every home and for sale in every country store. Potters in many small villages had only a small foot treadle to fashion jugs, jars, crocks, mugs, bean pots, and butter churns.

Liquids purchased from the grocer were poured into the buyer's jugs for the trip home and crocks were used for storing produce, dried foods, and root crops.

The making of earthenware articles in the various potteries was an involved process that required skill and patience on the part of the potter. The potter chose his clays very carefully and through many years of experience was able to mix the proper amount of water with the clay to form a thick uniform mixture. The clay was stored out of the weather in a place where the moisture content would remain stable. After the piece was turned and formed on the potter's wheel it was dried. A wood-fired kiln was used to bake the clay, often for as long as twenty-four to seventy-two hours. The finished pottery was not removed from the kiln until it cooled down. The pebbly glaze that appears on most stoneware pieces was applied by throwing salt into the kiln.

TEXT CONTINUED ON PAGE ONE HUNDRED THIRTY-FOUR

Plate 119. Schotten's "roasted coffees" and "ground spices" bin, circa 1900, made of poplar wood. Many such bins were made of pine or oak. Most of them date from approximately the same period. They were distributed to grocers who stocked the company's products.

Plate 120. Tippecanoe Mills Roasted Coffee bin, which dates from the period 1890–1910. Tin coffee bins such as this are not as common as wooden bins. The detailed tole painting on the bin makes it an exceptionally fine piece.

Plate 121. Cast iron stove with miniature utensils, circa 1875.

Plate 122. Cast iron child's stove, circa 1880.

Plate 123. Late 19th century doll carriage with wooden wheels.

Plate 124. Wooden blocks and horn.

Plate 125. Wooden rocking horse with original mane and tail, 19th century.

Plate 126. Guernsey cow on iron wheels, early 20th century.

There were few earthenware or stoneware potters prior to the nineteenth century. The finest examples of stoneware crocks, jugs, churns, and jars were produced in Ohio, New York, Pennsylvania, and New England, although there were many potteries throughout the country that turned out earthenware products on a large scale.

Stone grey crockery was usually stenciled or etched with the pottery's name, its location, and the size of the crock or jug. Jugs and crocks that carry additional decorations of birds or animals are especially collectable today. Early stoneware pieces were decorated with designs in cobalt blue. Later pieces were stenciled at the pottery rather than decorated by hand with original and unusual designs.

Plate 127. Toy horse pull-toy on iron wheels, circa 1910.

The American country or general store of the 19th century stocked toys of all kinds. Until about 1875 most of the toys sold in the United States were imported from Europe. Germany and Austria were prime sources for toys of all kinds.

American toy manufacturers offered little real competition until the 20th century. The materials used, for the most part, were wood, tin, and eventually cast iron.

Nineteenth-century toys are valuable today because of their scarcity. Then, as now, when a toy was broken it was discarded with but few tears. All toys in all ages have been subject to much use and abuse. Their life span was ephemeral and no thought was given to their preservation.

Plate 128. Cast iron train, mechanical tin doll, and circus wagon.

Cast iron mechanical banks and other 19th-century toys are now being reproduced abundantly, and in many cases they are being made from the original molds that were used in the late 19th century!

The toys shown in Plates 121–128 were photographed through the courtesy of Craig and Michael Raycraft.

Figure 14. Dated stoneware milk pitcher. This is a unique piece inasmuch as dated stoneware is seldom found. Pitchers of this type and similar jugs, crocks, and mugs were popular throughout the 19th century.

BIBLIOGRAPHY

This selective list of references represents a basic library that will enhance the appreciation and knowledge of any collector of early American folk and country antiques. Reading and rereading these books will provide endless enjoyment and continually whet ones interest in the furnishings of a century ago.

ANDREWS, EDWARD DEMING AND FAITH. *Shaker Furniture*. New York: Dover Publications, Inc., 1950. The best single book in print on the work of the Shakers. Beautifully illustrated with the finest examples of the Shaker craft.

CHRISTENSEN, ERWIN. *Index of American Design*. New York: The Macmillan Company, 1950. Outstanding book that provides a cross section of early American antiques. Includes chapters and color illustrations of folk art, toys, lighting fixtures, textiles, and furniture. Informative and well written.

GAMON, ALBERT. *Pennsylvania Country Antiques*. Englewood Cliffs: Prentice-Hall, Inc., 1968. The best aspect of this book is the section on dating antiques. Provides charts and dating procedures that are most valuable. Provides some insight into the Pennsylvania antiques that the collector may still find.

GOULD, MARY EARLE. *Early American Wooden Ware*. Rutland, Vt.: Charles E. Tuttle Company, 1962. Perhaps the best known of the writers of books on early Americana. Her books on tin and tole ware and early American houses are also considered classics. The wooden ware book is the only authoritative book in print on the subject. It would be impossible today to duplicate the collection she displays through countless pictures.

HAYWARD, ARTHUR. *Colonial Lighting*. New York: Dover Publications, Inc., 1962. An informally written book that was first published in 1923. The author covers the whole range of early American lighting. He also has numerous anecdotes about some of the items illustrated that are worth the price of the book.

KOVEL, RALPH AND TERRY. *American Country Furniture, 1780–1875*. New York: Crown Publishers, Inc., 1965. Excellent book for dating antique furniture. Probably the best book in print for collectors looking for pictures and approximate dates of pieces.

SLOANE, ERIC. *A Reverence for Wood*. New York: Funk and Wagnall's, 1965. Interesting and beautifully illustrated book that provides the reader with much factual information about early New England methods of construction and wood working. Sloane has written a series of books on Americana that should be a part of every collector's library.

INDEX